1C

DO ON THE WISCONSIN GREAT RIVER ROAD

CHRIS DINESEN ROGERS

NORM ROGERS

ISBN: 1469920565
ISBN-13: 978-1469920566

Printed in the U.S.A.

Second Edition

DEDICATION

We took my mother on a trip on the Wisconsin Great River Road in 2004. Being the devout Catholic that she was, I knew she would be overjoyed to see the Dickeyville Grotto. She was like a child going to the fair on that horribly hot, humid day we visited it. I'll never forget her being so excited to rush out of the car to see the beauty of the grotto herself. It is one of my most enduring images of the Wisconsin Great River Road.

We humbly dedicate this book to Pauline Orban, 1923-2005

CONTENTS

DISCLAIMER:

A Word to the Wise Traveler: Because events and places are constantly changing along the Wisconsin Great River Road, today's traveler would be wise to check local calendars for up-to-date information and website for current status. Although the authors exhausted every resource to get accurate information, they cannot be responsible for business closings or event changes. However, if you do find something amiss, please share your experience with us at 101Wisconsin.weborglodge.com.

Safe travels!

Cover Photo by Bob Nichols, USDA Natural Resources
Conservation Service

PREFACE

Centuries ago, huge ice sheets covered half of North America. As the climate warmed, colossal torrents of meltwaters rushed southward, carving what we now call the Mississippi River Valley. Words cannot describe the majesty or beauty left by the hand of Nature.

Over the bluffs on the east, fabulous sunrises are an everyday occurrence. On the west side in Iowa, equally impressive sunsets are just as common. Between the bluffs, dozens of species of waterfowl, upland game and aquatic life abound. Few places show more vividly the handiwork and diversity of Nature.

When Europeans populated this area, they built villages, towns and cities. Connecting these communities, they built roads and highways. In 1938, Congress appointed the Mississippi River Parkway Planning Commission to develop the the Great River Road.

Today, the Great River Road stretches over 2,300 miles down both sides of the river from Canada to the Gulf of Mexico. The Wisconsin section covers 250 miles, going through 33 river towns. In 2000, the Wisconsin Great River Road received the National Scenic Byway designation. There are thousands of things to do on the Wisconsin Great River Road. Here are just 101 of them.

Waymarking is mentioned throughout the book for a way to pack some more fun into your trip. Waymarking is like a GPS scavenger hunt that identifies locations of interest or historical importance. It includes sites such as historical markers, landmarks and unusual natural features. It is a great way to find an areas most unique spots. Go to http://www.waymarking.com for more information.

Prescott

1. Start your day in Prescott, Wisconsin. Pack the picnic basket and enjoy your lunch alfresco at Freedom Park. Prescott's largest park is located on a six-acre bluff overlooking the Mississippi and St. Croix Rivers. Admire the view and see the clear blue waters of the St. Croix meld into the muddy Mississippi. Viewing areas are open year-round. The grounds of the Great River Road Visitor and Learning Center at the park include several educational gardens. They also offer public programs. The hours vary seasonally.

Where: 200 Monroe Street, Prescott
Phone: 715-262-0104
Email: info@freedomparkwi.org
Website: http://www.freedomparkwi.org

Did you know?
Freedom Park was named for a rehabilitated bald eagle named "Freedom" that was released at the park in 1981.

2. Take a trip back in time as you follow the historic walking tour through Prescott's downtown where period buildings flank the main street. The Welcome and Heritage Center is located in the H.S. Miller Bank Building. Built in 1885, the center contains fascinating exhibits of local farming and river history and is on the National Register of Historic Places. Call for hours and more information.

Where: 233 Broad Street N.
Phone: 715-262-3284
Website: http://www.pressenter.com/~whctr/
Walking Tour: http://www.prescottwi.com/walktour.html

Follow the Great River Road Wine Tour with your first stop at the Valley Vineyard in Prescott. Their hobby-turned-business offers a variety of varietals, including the Marquette developed by the University of Minnesota. Valley Vineyard offers wines for sale and tasting. Open Wednesday through Sunday, 10 a.m. to 6 p.m.

Where: W10415 521st. Avenue, Prescott
Phone: 715-262-4235
Email: valley_vineyardltd@yahoo.com
Website: http://www.valleyvineyardltd.com

Did you know?
Prescott is the Wisconsin Great River Road's northernmost city. It is at this point that the road follows the Mississippi River into Minnesota and the Minnesota Great River Road. It is also the oldest river town on the Mississippi River.

3. After a long day of touring on the Great River Road, stop at the Muddy Waters Bar and Grill for a made-from-scratch dinner. The restaurant features three decks overlooking the Mississippi River. Enjoy a tropical libation as you watch the boats go by. The restaurant features live music on Sunday evenings.

Where: 231 N. Broad Street, Prescott
Phone: 715-262-5999
Website: http://www.muddywatersbarandgrill.com/

Did you know?
During the heyday of steamboat traffic, Prescott, like other towns on the Great River Road, was a center for transportation and milling. It is here where the St. Croix River and the Mississippi River meet.

4. Drive south from Prescott and marvel at the forested hills, valleys and bluffs. This section of the Wisconsin Great River Road is one of the most scenic drives in all of Wisconsin. You also have a unique opportunity to view the confluence of the St. Croix and Mississippi Rivers. The contrast between the clear waters of the St. Croix and the muddy Mississippi are obvious.

Did you know?
The St. Croix River was designated a National Scenic Riverway in 1968. It is one of just over one-quarter of one percent of the nation's rivers which are protected through this designation. It is one of the eight original rivers protected under the Wild and Scenic Rivers Act of 1968, signed into law by President Lyndon Johnson.

5. Keep your eyes open for the village of Diamond Bluff, named for this outstanding geological feature. Because of its prominence, it served as a navigation guide for river pilots traveling the Mississippi River. It is also the site of a tragic accident in the steamboat history when the steamboat, Sea Hawk, sank in 1890.

Where: Sea Hawk Memorial Park, Diamond Bluff

Did you know?
The park is a good place to relax and stretch your legs. You can fish or picnic here. There is also a sand beach

Bay City

6. Take in some local history at the River Bluffs History Center in Bay City. Operated by the Pierce County Historical Association, the center presents exhibits that chronicle the area's history   and historic church. The PCHA uses the center for special history exhibits. While there, visit the Conlin Log Cabin next door.

Where: W6321 E. Main Street, Bay City
Phone: Pierce County Historical Association 715-273-6611

Did you know?
The Great River Road is over 2,340 miles long and passes through or is bound by 10 states and two Canadian provinces. The Wisconsin section is 250 miles. The Mississippi River is the second longest river in the United States, second only to the Missouri River.

7. Stop at the Bow and Arrow historical marker just north of Bay City to see firsthand, one of "history's mysteries." Jacob Brower, of the Minnesota Historical Society, documented the site in 1902, describing it as a bow and arrow that was aimed to strike toward Lake Pepin. The Wisconsin Historical Society erected the historical marker in 1979. Did American Indians place the rock formation on a distant hillside? Does it actually depict a bow and arrow pointing to Lake Pepin? Is it a bird effigy? You decide!

Where: 1.1 miles south of U.S. 63 near Hager City, on the left side if you are traveling south.

Quick Facts: There is evidence all along the Great River Road of the mound-building cultures. In Wisconsin, the Eastern Woodland Indians built mounds from about 500 B.C. until the first European explorers arrived. Burial was the only purpose of the mounds. Effigy mounds represented local fauna such as birds, bears and turtles. When visiting these mounds, please use proper respect.

8. Pick your own berries and wildflowers at the many farms that dot the area. You can watch for signs along the road. If you need a pick-me-up, stop for a cup of joe and a treat for your sweet tooth at the Coffee By The Bay in Bay City. Hours are 8 a.m. to 5 p.m., closed Tuesdays and Wednesdays.

Where: W6518 State Hwy 35, Bay City
Phone: 715-594-3894
Email: laurie@coffeebythebay.net
Website: http://www.coffeebythebay.net/

Did you know?
Bay City was the setting for the first criminal trial in Pierce County, Wisconsin. When a man known as Mr. Morton tried to lay out a town plot, a squatter on the land, Mr. Dexter, objected and killed the surveyor. Mr. Morton continued his plan, calling the town, Saratoga, before it was changed to its present name, Bay City.

Maiden Rock

9. Take the "road less traveled" and head on down Rustic Road R-51, south of Maiden Rock. (You should watch for the brown Rustic Road sign.) This 4.3-mile gravel road winds through dense woodlands and bucolic farmlands, crosses trout streams and passes a historical church built in 1881 at the the intersection of 20th Avenue and County Highway CC. Beware of seasonal flooding on this road.

Where: Portion of 20th Avenue from County CC to County AA, Maiden Rock

The next stop on the wine tour is Vino in the Valley in Maiden Rock. The vineyard offers outdoor dining on Thursday and Saturday evenings as well as Sunday afternoons during the summer months. In the winter, visit the Vino in the Valley for a horse-drawn sleigh ride. They produce wines from six types of grapes, including their food-friendly white, Frontenac Gris. Open Thursdays from 5 p.m. to 10 p.m., Saturdays from 4 p.m. to 10 p.m. and Sundays from 12 p.m. to 7 p.m. Vino in the Valley also offers seasonal events.

Where: W3826 450th Avenue, Maiden Rock
Phone: 715-639-6677
Email: info@vinointhevalley.com
Website: http://www.vinointhevalley.com/

Did you know?
Created in 1973, the Rustic Road System of Wisconsin preserves the country roads of the state. To qualify for Rustic Road status, a road must have outstanding natural features, be lightly traveled and should be a closed loop to the highway. A rustic road's maximum speed limit is 45 mph.

10. Be sure and stop at the Maiden Rock historical marker and learn of the tragic legend behind the name. Erected in 1966, the marker tells of several versions of a story of an unfulfilled American Indian love affair. If you have a good set of binoculars, you can just make out the Minnesota Great River Road across the river.

Where: 3.1 miles south of County Highway AA, on the right if you are traveling south.

Did you know?
The village of Maiden Rock was once known as Harrisburg. It was named after the brothers, Amos and Albert Harris, who settled in the area in the 1850s. Later, the brothers sold their land to J.D. Trumbull. Trumbull changed the name to its present-day name, Maiden Rock, in keeping with the legend. He helped expand the village by adding a sawmill, grist and shingle mills. Trumbull and Harris constructed the first sail boat used for trade in 1856.

Stockholm

11. Don't forget to take some of the beauty of the Wisconsin Great River Road home with you. You can find your art treasure at the annual Stockholm Art Fair, held on the third Saturday of June. Over 100 artists from around the area display their works. Stroll the exhibits while enjoying live music and sampling treats from food vendors.

Where: Stockholm Village Park
Website: http://www.stockholmartfair.org/

For your next wine tour experience, head over to Maiden Rock Winery and Cidery. Their award-winning cider, made from European, English and North American cider apples, is sure to please. They offer tastings and tours as well as classes on how to make your own wine or cider. They are open Wednesday through Sunday, 10 a.m. to 6 p.m.

Where: W12266 King Lane, Stockholm
Phone: 715-448-3502
Email: info@maidenrockwinerycidery.com
Website: http://www.maidenrockwinerycidery.com/

Did you know?
Stockholm celebrated 150 years of Swedish heritage in September 2001. Founded in 1851, Stockholm is the oldest Swedish settlement in western Wisconsin and one of the smallest villages thriving in the state. Clamming and fishing provided a steady source of income in its early days. The village even grew carp commercially for export to New York.

12. End a day of sightseeing and touring at the Great River Bed and Breakfast in Stockholm. Built in 1854, this pioneer Swedish stone cottage features a large screened-in porch to take in the view and simply, just relax. For a bit of adventure, you can charter a 31-foot sailing sloop for a two-hour or longer excursion.

Where: W11976 State Highway 35, Stockholm
Phone: 1-800-657-4756
Website: http://www.greatriverbedandbreakfast.com

Did you know?
The Great River Bed and Breakfast was selected by *Midwest Living* magazine's June 1998 issue as one of their personal favorite "special places" in the Midwest. The inn is available between March and mid-December.

13. Take a bit of Wisconsin home with you. The Stockholm General features Wisconsin-made wines, beers and cheeses. You can grab a coffee or sandwich to go as you explore more of the Great River Road. You can also take care of the basic necessities if you are staying at one of the area's lodgings. Free Wi-Fi. Hours vary seasonally.

Where: N2030 Spring St. #4, Stockholm
Phone: 715-442-9077
Website: http://www.stockholmgeneral.com/

Quick Facts: Stockholm was honored with a royal visit by the Crown Prince Gustaf Aldof, Crown Princess Louise and Prince Bertil of Sweden on their way to the Twin Cities in 1938. The Crown Prince later recalled his trip to Stockholm, Wisconsin as "worth remembering."

14. Enjoy the superior craftsmanship of Amish-made goods at the Northern Oak Amish Furniture store. Find a one-of-a-kind piece made by local and Midwest craftsmen and artisans. You can also purchase certified stains to keep your furniture looking its best.

Where: N2048 Spring Street, Stockholm
Phone: 715-442-6008
Email: northern@northernoakamishfurniture.com
Website: http://northernoakamishfurniture.com/

Did you know?
As you leave Stockholm, keep an eye out for the Fort. St. Antoine historical marker. The marker commemorates the site of a French fort from the 17th century when the English and French fought for control of the region. Fort Antoine is also the name of the fictional town in the Mary Logue mysteries. Many of the Wisconsin Great River Road landmarks are mentioned in the books, giving you a unique experience to live the book you are reading.

Pepin

15. While you are in Pepin, don't miss the Laura Ingall Wilder Historical Museum. The museum has displays about the author and pioneer life in western Wisconsin. Ms. Wilder was born on a nearby farm in 1867. A historical representation of her birthplace is located seven miles west of Pepin on County Road CC (Waymark Code: WM4K5T). Museum hours are 10 a.m. to 5 p.m. from May 15 through October 17, then Friday, Saturday, and Sunday until November 1.

Where: 306 3rd Street (Hwy 35), Pepin
Phone: 715-442-2142
Email: info@lauraingallspepin.com
Website: http://www.lauraingallspepin.com/

Did you know?
Laura Ingall Wilder published her first book, "*Little House in the Big Prairie*," in 1932 when she was 65 years old. The book describes her childhood in the Pepin area in the 1870s. The overwhelming success of her books surprised Ms. Wilder, who once said, "I had no idea I was writing history."

16. Find yourself in a pickle--literally! Dine at the Pickle Factory Restaurant or have a drink at the Bottom of the Barrel Pub, open during the weekends in the summer. Both are located in the old Pepin Pickling Company building. The pickling operation began in 1904 and continued until 1937. The restaurant's signature appetizer is, of course, its deep-fried pickles. Summer hours: open at 11 a.m., Monday through Friday. Open at 8:30 a.m. on Saturdays and Sundays. Call for other times.

Where: 250 First Street, Pepin
Phone: 715-442-4400
Email: blohman@centurytel.net
Website: http://www.pepinpicklefactory.com/

Did you know?
Pepin County became part of Wisconsin as part of a treaty with the Dakota Indian nation in 1837. The Dakota subsisted on bison and other local produce. Pierre Esprit Radisson, an early French explorer, referred to them as the "Nation of the Beef."

17. You can take in the arts and fine craftsmanship at the T. & C. Latané and BNOX Gold and Iron Art Gallery in Pepin. Both shops offer Midwest-inspired items to bring a bit of the Wisconsin Great River Road home with you. T. & C. Latané is open Fridays and Saturdays, May to December. BNOX has variable seasonal hours. While at BNOX, ask about the BNOX mystery.

T. & C. Latané
Where: 412 2nd Street, Pepin
Phone: 715-442-2419
Email: tlatane@centurytel.net
Website: http://www.spaco.org/latane/tclourshop.htm

BNOX
Where: 404 First Street, Pepin
Phone: 715-442-2201
Email: info@bnoxgold.com
Website: http://www.bnoxgold.com/

Did you know?
The towns of Pepin and Stockholm are a renaissance home for many artists and artisans, looking for inspiration in the area's fabulous views and vistas. With the bluffs along the Mississippi River, they have plenty of nature-inspired material.

18. You can take the kids trout fishing at Pine Hill Springs Trout & Trails near Pepin. No fishing license is required. Pine Hill provides the gear, and you catch the fish. They'll even clean and ice your catch for the trip home. They are open year-round. Call ahead to check seasonal hours.

Where: W9194 Cross Rd, Pepin
Phone: 715-442-4700

Did you know?
Lake Pepin was originally called the Lake of Tears. Father Louis Hennepin and two lay Frenchmen, Anthony Augelle and Michael Accault, explored the area by canoe in 1680. French trappers and traders used the area extensively for the years following, holding off British attempts to become part of the trade.

19. Grab your sketchbook, pack the easel and get inspired! Lake Pepin was one of many sites that captivated the painters of the Hudson River School, a group of artists that defined American landscape painting. The lake was made famous by Laura Ingall Wilder's book, "*Little House in the Big Woods.*"

Did you know?
William Cullen Bryant was a famous writer and patron of the Hudson River School artists. Upon visiting the area, he was quoted as saying that Lake Pepin "....should be visited in the summer by every poet and painter in the land."

20. You can boat, canoe or kayak on the widest spot on the Mississippi River, Lake Pepin. Formed by the delta of the Wisconsin's Chippewa River, the lake is 22 miles long and 2.5 miles wide. It is one of the most beautiful spots along the Mississippi River. Year-round fishing access is available. Rumors abound that Lake Pepin may have its own lake monster, which the locals call, Pepie. An alleged sighting from April 1871 was documented by the Minnesota Historical Society.

Pepie's Website: http://www.pepie.net/

Did you know?
Lake Pepin is the birthplace of waterskiing, invented by Ralph Samuelson from Lake City, MN. He fashioned his first skis from barrel staves before designing his own from lumber and leather strips as bindings.

21. When nothing less than a gourmet dinner will do, you can visit the nationally renowned Harbor View Cafe in Pepin. Seafood and Norwegian fare are specialties of the house. Its critically acclaimed menu features items that support sustainability and local growers. You can enjoy the breathtaking view of Lake Pepin as you dine in comfort. The restaurant is open Thursdays through Monday only.

Where: 314 First Street, Pepin
Phone: 715-442-3893
Email: harborviewpepin@gmail.com
Website: http://www.harborviewpepin.com/

Harbor View Cafe has been a Midwest tradition since 1980. Patrons regularly travel from the Twin Cities to regularly enjoy its made-from-scratch menu.

Nelson

22. For a true experience in solitude, take a walk on the wild side and visit the Tiffany Bottoms Wildlife Area in Nelson. This 13,000-acre refuge is a 10-mile stretch of virgin forest and backwater. Tiffany Bottoms offers numerous hiking and canoeing opportunities. Trails are not marked, but you are welcome to hike the area. Take along a GPS device or GPS-enabled smartphone to get back to the car.

Where: Located between the towns of Nelson and Durand
Phone: 608-685-6222
Website:
http://dnr.wi.gov/org/land/wildlife/wildlife_areas/tiffany.ht
m

Did you know?
The state-threatened Kentucky warbler is commonly found in the Tiffany Bottoms area in early summer.

23. You can spend a relaxing weekend in a rustic cabin or cottage at the Cedar Ridge Resort in Nelson. The resort features 300 feet of private shoreline. For the angler, you can enjoy river access and 14 and 16-foot Lund boat rentals. The pet-friendly resort is open year-round.

Where: S1376 Great River Road 35S, Nelson
Phone: 608-685-4998
Email: wesstensland@tds.net
Website: http://cedarridgeresort.com/

The Village without a Founder - Part 1
Local legend has it that James Nelson founded the village of Nelson, who settled in the area in 1843. Nelson dubbed the site, Nelson's Landing. It thrived as a shop for travelers. The history of what eventually become of James Nelson is lost, but the name stuck, with the village bearing its name today.

24. What is a trip to Wisconsin without bringing home some cheese? Enjoy the best of the state with a wine and cheeseboard in the Nelson Cheese Factory's Fireplace Wine Room. Grab a sandwich or soup for a delicious lunch on the pet-friendly patio. The store carries a wide selection of cheeses and imports from around the world. Open seven days a week, with seasonal hours.

Where: S237 State Road 35 South, Nelson
Phone: 715-673-4151
Website: http://www.nelsoncheese.com/

The Village without a Founder - Part 2
Local legend further reports that Madison Wright was the first permanent settler of Nelson. Though he lived in the Nelson area, he traded in Wabasha, Minnesota, which soon become his home. He seldom returned to Nelson. Years later, the Nelson town board received a bill for Madison Wright's funeral. The board responded that "...if Wright died penniless, it was because he spent all his money in Wabasha. Therefore, they should bury him."

25. You can find out what "80 Miles of Deals, Steals and Squeals" means. Be sure and drive the Great River Road from Alma to Bay City to take part in the longest garage sale in Wisconsin. The sale is held the first weekend in May. A picker's dream! Take a side trip to Winona, MN and make it an even 100 miles.

Did you know?
Alma began as a settlement for Swiss immigrants. In 1848, two young Swiss men began making a living by providing cut lumber to fuel the steamboats that traveled up and down the river. The two men liked the area, and the rest is history. At the Beef Slough historical marker a half mile north of Alma, you can learn about the area's rocky beginnings, Waymark Code: WM4CCB.

Alma

26. For the best homemade pies in the state as recognized by the Milwaukee Sentinel and the St. Paul Pioneer Press, visit the Alma Hotel Bar and Restaurant. The hotel features 11 rooms with both private and shared baths available. The restaurant features homemade items.

Where: 201 North Main Street, Alma
Phone: 608-685-3380

Get ready for something special at the Danzinger Winery in Alma. Their critically-acclaimed Crescent Moon wine, a refreshing unoaked white, won the 2011 Cold Climate Wine Competition. They are open daily 10 a.m. to 5 p.m. and closed on major holidays.

Where: S2015 Grapeview Lane, Alma
Phone: 608-685-6000
Email: info@danzingervineyards.com
Website: http://www.danzingervineyards.com/

Did you know?
A brewery provided the first source of industry for Alma. The theory was that beer helped men pass the long, cold winters--that along with a number of local cigar factories.

27. You have to see it to believe it. The entire town of Alma is only two streets wide and is so steep that one street is almost directly on top of the other. It's a town where "people go upstairs to their basement." Try walking at least one of the 10 staircases that connects Main Street with Second Street for a workout that will burn.

> *"The man who goes alone can start today; but he who travels with another must wait till that other is ready."*
> ~ Henry David Thoreau

28. Take a leisurely stroll through historic Alma, following the self-guided tour. Many of the homes and buildings are over 100 years old. Stop in the Alma Area Museum to see exhibits on local history. It is open Thursday through Sunday during the summer and Friday through Sunday during the fall. Admission is free.

Where: 505 South 2nd Street, Alma, located in the Buffalo County Training School & Teachers College
Phone: 608-685-4013
Email: society@almahistory.org
Website: http://www.almahistory.org/

Did you know?
All of downtown Alma is listed on the National Register of Historic Places. The town contains several historic homes, including the Ibach Mansion and the Tritsch House.

29. Take a guided houseboat tour of the Mississippi River backwaters in search of migratory waterfowl. You can also go birding by train. Maybe you can find one or more birds to add to your life list. This and dozens of other activities are scheduled for the annual Great River Birding and Nature Festival held the second week of May near Alma. Call the Wings Over Alma Nature and Art Center for more information at 608-685-3303.

Where: 118 N Main Street, Alma
Phone: 608-685-3303
Email: center@wingsoveralma.org
Website: http://wingsoveralma.org/

Did you know?
The open waters of Lock and Dam #4 make it a great place to view wintering bald eagles feeding from November to March. It offers good opportunities for capturing stunning photographs of our national bird.

30. See why Alma is considered one of Wisconsin's best bird watching hotspots. Attend the annual Swan Watch at Rieck's Lake in Alma. In late fall, literally thousands of migrating tundra swans pass through on their migratory journeys south.

Where: 3 miles north of Alma on Hwy. 35
Phone: 608-248-3499 (Info available between September to November only.)
Email: swanalma@mwt.net
Website: http://almaswanwatch.org/index.htm

Quick Facts: Tundra swans were once known as whistling swans. They were the most widespread of swans in North America. Tundra swans have a wingspan of six to seven feet and weigh upwards of 20 pounds. The endangered trumpeter swan is larger. It gets its name from its melodious trumpeting-like sound.

31. You don't have to own a boat to fish for walleye. Try your angling skills on the largest public fishing dock on the Mississippi River at the Great Alma Fishing Float. You can even enjoy some overnight fishing. Owners Jim and Tim Lodermeier can give you the insider information on the area's best fishing.

Where: River Street in Alma
Phone: Jim: 651-380-7296; Tim: 651-380-5322
Email: almafloat@yahoo.com
Website: http://www.almafishingfloat.com/

Did you know?
The scientific name for walleye, *Stizostedion vitreum*, gives you some interesting clues about one of Wisconsin's prized game fish. The genus name, *Stizostedion*, means "pungent throat." The species name, *vitreum*, means glassy, referring to its large eyes that help it locate its prey.

32. Get a birds-eye view of the Wisconsin Great River Road at Buena Vista Park. Located 500 feet above Alma and the Mississippi River Valley, the park is a natural viewing platform for watching the annual raptor migration. It also provides a fabulous view of the sand islands and backwater areas of the Mississippi River. It is a great visual geology lesson of the Mississippi River. Pack a lunch and picnic at the park.

Where: County Road E from Main Street in Alma and then, up the bluff to the park
For Information: 608-685-3330
Website:
http://www.wingsoveralma.org/visitalmathecenter/buenavist aparktrail.html

Quick Facts: *Better Home and Gardens* magazine named Buena Vista Park as "one of the river valley's finest natural balconies."

33. Enjoy art crafted by local artists at the Art and Soul Gallery. The gallery features original artwork and mission-based imports. From there, head on over to Soul Sisters where the emphasis is on local with local art and goods. Get inspired with the artists' pottery, jewelry and paintings. The galleries have seasonal hours. Call for more information.

Art and Soul Gallery
Where: 303 N. Main Street, Alma
Phone: 715-448-2049 (Gail, Artist)
Email: gailkp@centurytel.net
Website: http://www.art-soul.org/

Soul Sisters
Where: 409 N. Main Street, Alma
Phone: 608-685-3700
Email: soulsistersart@gmail.com
Website: http://www.soulsistersart.com/

Quick Fact: The Mississippi River is the largest river in the United States, based on volume.

Fountain City

34. Spend a lazy relaxing day on the river to recharge your battery. Rent a kayak at River City Kayaks in Fountain City. Get an up-close view of the Mississippi Rivers and its stunning views. Don't forget the suntan lotion!

Phone: 608-687-1250

Did you know?
Fountain City is the oldest settlement in Buffalo County. The name refers to the numerous springs in the nearby hills.

35. Bird watchers, grab your checklists and binoculars! Explore the backwaters and marshes of Buffalo City, located five miles north of Fountain City. It provides excellent viewing opportunities of a variety of ducks, loons, rails and herons. The area also supplies habitat for pelicans, ospreys, cranes and egrets. This can be just your chance to identify an elusive wading bird. You can stretch your legs with a leisurely stroll on the one-mile nature trail at Foelsch River Side Park.

Did you know?
Great egrets were hunted almost to extinction for their elegant breeding plumes. For a time, the plumes that adorned hats and clothing were all the fashion rage. Ginger Rogers can be seen wearing a gown of egret plumes in the movie, "*Top Hat.*"

36. Visit the Rock in the House, featured in *People* magazine and on the *Today Show*. The name of the tourist attraction is for the house that got in the way of a two-story boulder falling from the nearby bluffs in Fountain City. Hours are Monday through Saturday from 10 a.m. to 6 p.m., and Sunday from 1 to 5 p. The site is closed during the winter months. Call before visiting to verify hours. Waymark Code: WM24M8

Where: 440 North Shore Dr., Fountain City
Phone: 608-687-3553

Quick Fact: The incident that gave the Rock in the House its name wasn't the first time the structure met with rocky times. In 1901, a boulder smashed through the Dubler home, killing Mrs. Dubler. The present-day garage stands where the Dubler house once stood.

37. Check out the highest point on the Mississippi River bluffs at Eagle Bluff near Fountain City. The 550-foot bluff commands a breathtaking view of the surrounding area. For a rare treat, visit the park during the months of March and April to view hundreds of migrating turkey vultures.

Quick Fact: Fountain City was settled in 1839. Its population base reflects its northern European influences.

38. For authentic Irish fare that can't be beat, have lunch in one of Fountain City's historic buildings, the Monarch Public House. First established in 1894, the pub includes the hand-tooled oak backbar from this era. The roast beef sandwich is out of this world. The tavern also brews its own beer under the Fountain City Brewing Company, Inc. label. Hours are Friday through Tuesday from 11 a.m. to close, Wednesday and Thursdays, 4 p.m. To close. From December 1 through April 30, Monarch Public House is closed on Tuesdays.

Where: 19 N. Main Street, Fountain City
Phone: 608-687-4231
Email: monarch@monarchpublichouses.com
Website: http://www.monarchtavern.com/

Quick Facts: The Monarch Public House was voted one of the top 12 favorite restaurants on the Upper Mississippi River, "Big River" magazine July 2002 and added as a recommended travel destination by *Gourmet* magazine in July 2009.

39. When you are in Fountain City, take a detour on the surrounding back roads and visit the Prairie Moon Sculpture Gardens outside of Fountain City. The site features nearly 40 sculptures created by the late Herman Rusch, folk artist. The gardens are open Sunday afternoons during May to October. Call to verify hours before visiting. Waymark Code: WM24KZ

Where: S-2727 Prairie Moon Road, Fountain City
Phone: 608-687-9874

The next stop on the wine tour takes you to Seven Hawks Vineyards in Fountain City. It features a tasting room and wine bar to enjoy their selection of hand-crafted wines. Their wines are made from locally-grown grapes and fruits. They are open Monday through Saturday from 11 a.m. to 7 p.m. and Sundays from 12 p.m. to 6 p.m.

Where: 17 North Street, Fountain City
Phone: 1-866-946-3741
Email: wines@sevenhawksvineyards.com
Website: http://www.sevenhawksvineyards.com/

Did you know?
When traveling through this area, keep an eye out for albino deer. Albino deer are so rare that they are designated a protected mammal in Wisconsin and in other states. The Fountain City area has more albino deer than any place else in the world.

40. For a delectable seafood fest, have dinner at a local institution, the Hillside Fish House. Originally called the Marshland House, the restaurant was established in 1855 and has been in continuous operation since. The menu features a wide variety of seafood-based appetizers and entrees. Go all out and enjoy its signature Hurricane Platter for two, which includes king crab, shrimp, scallops and wine. Reservations are strongly recommended.

Where: W126 State Road 35/54, Fountain City
Phone: 608-687-6141
Website: http://www.hillsidefishhouse.com/

Quick Fact: The Hillside Fish House was a warming stop for travelers following the wagon bridge to Winona, MN.

41. Looking for a place to camp? Check out Merrick State Park, nestled in the bluffs near Fountain City. You can relax and enjoy the tranquil backwaters of the Mississippi River. The Merrick TURTLES, a non-profit group, offers canoeing, fishing, hiking and sponsored naturalist programs.

Where: S2965 State Road 35, Fountain City
Phone: 608-687-4936
Website:
http://www.dnr.state.wi.us/org/land/parks/specific/merrick

Did you know?
The Fountain City and Cochrane area is located within the Great Northern Flyway for migratory birds. Thousands of waterfowl use the flyway for their annual migrations. In fact, the flyway provides habitat for 40 percent of the nation's migratory waterfowl!

Trempealeau

42. Wildlife-watching opportunities galore await you the Trempealeau National Wildlife Refuge, north of Centerville. You can take the four-mile Prairie Edge Tour Loop drive, which includes a stop at an observation deck and 11 stops to learn more about the sand prairie, backwater marsh, and hardwood forest that make up the site.

Where: W28488 Refuge Road, Trempealeau
Phone: 608-539-2311
Website: http://www.fws.gov/midwest/Trempealeau/

Quick Fact: The impressive species list of the Trempealeau National Wildlife Refuge includes 60 mammal species, 30 reptile species and 25 species of fish. A complete bird checklist is available from the U.S. Geological Survey at: http://www.npwrc.usgs.gov/resource/birds/chekbird/r3/trempeal.htm

43. The *Milwaukee Journal-Sentinel* called the Trempealeau Hotel's food and atmosphere "...well worth savoring." You will too. Enjoy the ambiance of waterfront dining, with a menu that has something for everyone. Vegetarians will love its famous Walnut Burger. The hotel offers lodging in one of its guestrooms or luxury suites.

Where: 11332 Main Street, Trempealeau
Phone: 608-534-6898
Email: info@trempealeauhotel.com
Website: http://www.trempealeauhotel.com/
Website: http://www.walnutburger.com/

Did you know?
The Trempealeau Hotel is one of the few buildings to survive a devastating fire in 1888 that engulfed the original riverfront business district. Teams of horses moved the hotel and other surviving structures to their present-day location.

44. You can learn the fascinating history of the Hopewell Indian cultures and explore the handiwork of a geological masterpiece at the Perrott State Park in Trempealeau. You should make sure and see Mount Trempealeau, the "...mountain whose foot is bathed by water," near the visitor center. This geological anomaly is actually a solid rock island that is as high as the neighboring bluffs.

Where: W26247 Sullivan Road, Trempealeau
Phone: 608-534-6409
Website:
http://www.dnr.state.wi.us/org/land/parks/specific/perrot/

Quick Fact: In the 1850s, a Methodist minister wrote that Trempealeau was believed to be the original Garden of Eden. With its bluffs and abundant wildlife, no place on Earth seemed more fitting a location.

45. Visit historic downtown Trempealeau, where the entire two blocks are listed on the National Register of Historic Places. Nearby, you should be sure and visit historic McGilvray Road in Van Loon Wildlife area, also known as the McGilvray Bottoms, to see the five-steel bowstring, arch-truss bridges. Just east of Trempealeau, you can view a historical marker that commemorates the first five-mile stretch of the Mississippi River Parkway, Waymark Code: WM4CAA.

Website: http://www.7bridgesrd.org/index.html

Quick Fact: The National Register of Historic Places is the official list of cultural resources worthy of preservation, as authorized under the National Historic Preservation Act of 1966. The National Park Service administers the register. To qualify, a place must have significant historical, cultural, archaeological or architectural value. The place must have played an important role in the history or people of the past.

46. Music lovers will find a venue for any taste in Trempealeau. Reggae lovers won't want to miss the Reggae Sunsplash, held in May. For the perfect summer evening, check out the Stars Under the Stars Concert Series at the Trempealeau, featuring national acts. In June, you'll want to plan a trip to see the concert grounds for the Blues Bash. Call the Trempealeau Hotel for details.

Phone: 608-534-6898

The final stop on your Great River Road wine tour is the Elmaro Vineyard in Trempealeau. With the first vines planted in 2006, the winery features a variety of specialty wines, including its Fire of 1888 Reserve that commemorates the tragedy of that year. Join them for a private sunset tasting or a Romantic Rendezvous wine and food tasting. Hours: Wednesday and Thursday, 12 p.m. to 5 p.m., Friday and Saturday, 12 p.m. to 7 p.m., Sunday, 12 p.m. to 6 p.m. Monday and Tuesday by appointment.

Where: N14756 Delaney Rd. Trempealeau, WI
Phone: 608-534-6456
Website: http://www.elmarovineyard.com/

Quick Fact: The state dance of Wisconsin is the polka, adopted in 1993.

47. Pack a lunch, and hit the bike trails! Trempealeau is a cycling paradise. Choose from several routes, ranging from 10 to 40 miles that beckon riders of every skill level. The trails lead past river views, buffalo farms, prairies and bluffs.

Did you know?

The topography of "Coulee Country" was formed by an event that didn't happen. Glaciers missed the area, and so evolved what is now known as the Driftless Area.

48. Anglers, test the waters at Lake Onalaska. The lake offers year-round fishing. It's just what you'd expect from a place known as the Sunfish Capitol of the World. The lake is over 8,300 acres, with a maximum depth of 40 feet. In addition to panfish, you can also fish for largemouth bass, smallmouth bass, Northern pike and walleye. The lake has eight boat landings.

Website:
http://www.wisconsinslakes.com/la%20crosse_county_lakes.html

Did you know?
Unlike many lakes in Wisconsin, Lake Onalaska is an artificial lake. The Army Corps of Engineers created it in 1937 during the construction of Lock and Dam #7.

49. Sample one of Trempealeau's famous catfish sandwiches supplied by local fishermen during Catfish Days, held the week after Fourth of July weekend. Join the fun, with music, dancing, games and a fishing tournament. For bicyclists, join in the Trempealeau County Bike Club's Catfish 50 Tour.

Side Trip: If trout fishing is more your style, the Trempealeau area has several cold water trout streams. Brook trout are common. A Wisconsin fishing license or stamp is required.

50. For fun and sun, bike the Great River Trail. Beginning in Onalaska, this 24-mile crushed limestone trail winds through pine forests and prairies. You can see one of the largest Indian mounds in the area. The trail is part of the Mississippi River Trail that follows the entire length of the river from Minnesota to Louisiana. The Great River Trail lies within the Mississippi Flyway. You'll have plenty of opportunities to do some birdwatching on a cycling break, especially during the spring and fall migrations.

Website:
http://dnr.wi.gov/org/land/parks/specific/greatriver/

FYI: You must purchase a state of Wisconsin bike pass to use any of the public bike trails. Daily passes are available at any Wisconsin Department of Natural Resources office and at trailheads in many areas.

Onalaska

51. Immerse yourself in the lumber history of Onalaska at the Onalaska Area Historical Society Museum. Informative displays chronicle Onalaska's early days as a lumber mill boomtown. It also has exhibits that give a glimpse into 19th century life as well as archaeological artifacts. The museum is located in the public library. It is open Wednesday through Friday from 1 to 3 p.m. It can also be viewed by appointment for groups.

Where: 741 Oak Ave. S., Museum Suite, Onalaska
Phone: 608-781-9568

Did you know?
Onalaska gets its name from the line in the Thomas Campbell's poem, "*The Pleasures of Hope.*" The line recalls the plaintive cry of the wolf, "The wolf's long howl from Onalaska's shore..."

52. Give something back to the Great River Road. Take part in the Great River Trail Clean-Up, sponsored by the Holmen Area Foundation.

Phone: 608-526-1320

Quick Fact: Onalaska is believed to be an Aleut word, "dwelling together harmoniously."

La Crosse

53. Experience a bit of culture at the Pump House Regional Arts Center in La Crosse. Once the city's first water pump house, the center is now host to a variety of art shows and exhibits, many with a Midwest flavor. It is also a resource for area artists and contains three visual art galleries. It is open Tuesday through Saturday.

Where: 119 King Street, La Crosse
Phone: 608-785-1434
Email: contact@thepumphouse.org
Website: http://thepumphouse.org/

Quick Facts: The original pump house was built in 1880. During its height, it pumped 2.5 million gallons of water a day. Today, the pump house is listed on the State and National Registers of Historic Places.

54. You haven't fully experienced Wisconsin until you get your very own Cheddarhead, exclusively from TJ Cheddarhead's Wisconsin Gift Shop in La Crosse. The Cheddarhead was voted "Wisconsin's Best Souvenir!" by *Wisconsin Trails* magazine.

Where: 215 Pearl Street, La Crosse
Phone: 608-784-8899
Website: http://www.cheddarheads.com/

Fun Fact: The owners of Cheddarheads report that they have received photos of customers wearing their Cheddarhead t-shirts in Scotland, Saudi Arabia, Japan, Hawaii, Africa, Russia, Bora Bora, England, the Great Wall of China, the Aztec ruins in Mexico and even during the dismantling of the Berlin Wall. The distinctive cheddarhead was created in 1986.

55. Rent a canoe and follow the 5-mile Long Lake Canoe Trail at the Upper Mississippi River National Wildlife and Fish Refuge. Even for the beginner, the looped trail only takes about three to four hours. It is the finest way to experience this wildlife haven. The entire refuge encompasses 261 river miles from Wabasha, MN to Rock Island, IL. Keep your eyes peeled to view any of the refuge's 250-plus eagle nests, 5,000 heron and egret nests or 360 species of birds.

Where: 51 E. Fourth St. Room 101, Winona, MN (District Office)
Phone: 507-452-4232
Website:
http://www.fws.gov/midwest/UpperMississippiRiver/

Quick Facts: The Upper Mississippi River National Wildlife and Fish Refuge encompass 200,000 acres. About half of the world's population of canvasback ducks uses the refuge for habitat.

56. Discover historic downtown La Crosse, named by the editors of *Wisconsin Trails* magazine as the "Best Revitalized Downtown in the State of Wisconsin." Buildings dating back to 1866 provide character and charm for one of the largest commercial historic districts in Wisconsin. Many unique shops and antique stores await you.

Did you know?
The National Trust for Historic Preservation awarded La Crosse the 2002 Great American Main Street Award for its successful efforts in downtown revitalization through historic preservation.

57. Count the lederhosen during Oktoberfest, held the last week of September in La Crosse. Festival activities include carnival rides, arts and craft shows and ethnic foods. Authentic German bands provide the "oompah" music.

Website: http://www.oktoberfestusa.com

Did you know?
The tradition of Oktoberfest goes back to the wedding celebration of Princess Therese to Bavarian Crown Prince Ludwig in 1810. The La Crosse Oktoberfest celebration began in 1961. It is one of the few authentic Old World folk festivals in the United States.

58. Drive the switchback roads to the top of Granddad's Bluff in La Crosse, voted by the readers of *Wisconsin Trails* magazine as the most scenic view in the state. On a clear day, you can see three states--Wisconsin, Iowa and Minnesota. The site has picnic areas, a shelter house and coin-operated binoculars so you can take in the view.

Where: 400 La Crosse Street, La Crosse

Did you know?
Granddad Bluff almost became a large-scale quarrying operation were it not for the loud objections of the La Crosse residents in the early 1900s. They raised money with the help of a local prominent family, Joseph and Irene Hixon, to secure the necessary funds to purchase the land and donate it to the city as a park.

59. Travel on the Wisconsin Great River Road on any sunny winter day to catch a glimpse of soaring bald eagles. The open waters of the Mississippi River provide prey and habitat for wintering birds. On a good day, it is possible to see hundreds of eagles. Any open water on the river is a good place for viewing them.

Quick Facts: Eagles are probably the largest soaring raptor you'll see. To identify bald eagles in the air, look for the characteristic white head and tail denoting the adult bird. If you see a large bird soaring over water, chances are that it is an eagle. Eagles hold their wings straight in flight, unlike vultures that soar with their wings in a V-shape.

60. Attention all duffers: Play the oldest golf course in western Wisconsin. The over 100-year old Forest Hills Golf Course is nestled at the foot of Granddad's Bluff in La Crosse. The bluffs add an extra bit of challenge with elevation changes on various holes. The amenities include a golf shop and banquet facilities. Golfers have enjoyed the site since 1892.

Where: 600 Losey Boulevard N., La Crosse
Phone: 608-779-GOLF
Email: info@foresthillsgolf.org
Website: http://www.foresthillsgolf.org/

Quick Fact: The Forest Hills Golf Course is one of the original seven courses to form the Wisconsin State Golf Association in the early 1900s.

61. When in La Crosse, have dinner in a National Historic site. The Freighthouse Restaurant was voted "Best Restaurant" by *Where the Locals Eat.* The specialty of the house is its slow-roasted prime rib. After supper, relax by the fireplace and enjoy live entertainment on Fridays and Saturdays. The restaurant opens at 5 p.m. daily.

Where: 107 Vine Street, La Crosse
Phone: 608-784-6211
Website: http://freighthouserestaurant.com/

But, wait, there's more: If that isn't enough to convince you that it is worth the stop, the Freighthouse Restaurant was praised by the *La Crosse Tribune* for its Readers' Choice Award for Best Restaurant, Best Steaks, Best Seafood, Best Wine Selection, Best Salad Bar and Best Bar.

62. Learn how archaeologists process artifacts and other finds from nearby project sites. The Mississippi River Valley Archaeology Center at the University of Wisconsin-La Crosse offers activities and workshops or all ages. Participate in archaeological field work. Learn about local cultures. Tour a local excavation site. Some programs have fees and require reservations.

Where: 1725 State Street, La Crosse
Phone: 608-785-8463
Email: bjancik@uwlax.edu
Website: http://www.uwlax.edu/mvac/index.htm

Did you know?
If you were traveling the Wisconsin Great River Road about 12,000 years ago, you would see woolly mammoths, mastodons, caribou and maybe even a six-foot long giant beaver.

63. Share a malt and fries with your best girl at Rudy's in La Crosse. The authentic 1950s drive-in features roller skating carhops. Every Tuesday night from June until September is cruise-in night when owners of vintage automobiles stop in for freshly-brewed root beer. It is the largest in the Midwest. Join the fun! Be sure and visit Rudy's website for coupons and specials.

Where: 1004 La Crosse Street, La Crosse
Phone: 608-782-2200
Email: gary@rudysdrivein.com
Website: http://www.rudysdrivein.com/

Quick Facts: La Crosse has a long history as a happening place. One of its most famous residents was William Frederick "Buffalo Bill" Cody. The legendary scout and showman put on theatrical plays at the Opera House. Buffalo Bill brought his Wild West Show to the city several times.

64. For the best ribs around, stop at Piggy's Restaurant in La Crosse, where they "overlook nothing but the Mississippi." The delectable menu features exclusive smokehouse entrees and an extensive wine list. Piggy's has been the winner of *Wine Spectator's* Award of Excellence since 1998.

Where: 501 Front Street South, La Crosse
Phone: 608-784-4877
Email: ribs@piggys.com
Website: http://www.piggys.com/

Did you know?
Buffalo Bill Cody's many accomplishments did not end with his Wild West Show. Cody and one of his friends, Dr. David Powell, patented at least four medical remedies together.

65. Winter sports reign supreme at Mount La Crosse! With over 19 slopes and three lifts, the site offers plenty of skiing excitement. Want to improve your skills? Mount La Crosse offers private skiing lessons for children and adults. Afterward, warm up at the St. Bernard Room, named the Best Skier Bar in the Midwest by *Skiing* magazine.

Where: Look for the sign near the junction of Highways 14/61 on Highway 35
Phone: 608-788-0044 or 1-800-426-3665
Email: info@mtlacrosse.com
Website: http://www.mtlacrosse.com

Quick Facts: Mount La Crosse has slopes for every skill level from the gentle Mileaway Slope to the sheer excitement of Damnation, mid-America's steepest trail. The Mileaway Slope is Wisconsin's longest slope.

66. Indulge yourself in luxury. Formerly the Mons Anderson House, the Chateau offers French and Mediterranean cuisine. Chef and owner Timothy Ewers, worked under Jean Christophe Novelli, a four Michelin-star awarded French chef. You can also take a tour of this 1854 mansion. The elegant house has stunning woodwork throughout. There are six original marble fireplaces and 18 rooms, including seven splendid guestrooms. Closed Sundays. Reservations are strongly encouraged.

Where: 410 Cass Street La Crosse
Phone: 608-782-6498
Email: chefTim@lechateaulacrosse.com
Website: http://lechateaulacrosse.com/

Quick Facts: Built in 1854, the Mons Anderson House is listed on the National Register of Historic Places. The mansion was restored in 1982 at a cost of $1.3 million. In 1986, it earned the Honor Award from the Wisconsin Society of Architects.

67. Explore the bounds of your imagination at The Children's Museum in La Crosse. The museum is filled with exhibits that allow children to pretend and discover the world around them. Be a firefighter or a police officer. Play dress up. Climb the 28-foot Mount LeKid climbing wall. The museum has a daily event schedule. It's fun for the entire family! Closed Mondays and major holidays.

Where: 207 Fifth Avenue South, La Crosse
Phone: 608-784-2652
Email: info@funmuseum.org
Website: http://funmuseum.org/

"It's never too late to be what you might have been."
~George Eliot

68. Take in one of La Crosse's 42 city parks. Stroll or bike the river walk overlooking the Mississippi River to see the confluence of the three rivers--Mississippi River, Black River and La Crosse River. If hiking is more your speed, visit Hixon Forest Nature Center, the second largest city park in Wisconsin.

Where: 2702 Quarry Road, La Crosse
Phone: 608-784-0303

Did you know?
Its strategic location at the confluence of these three rivers helped La Crosse prosper as a mill town. The confluence is considered a sacred place in some American Indian cultures. Nothing bad was believed to happen at such a unique place.

69. For a bit of culture, take a sculpture tour in La Crosse. Five impressive sculptures can be found throughout the city: the Hiawatha Sculpture at the confluence of the Mississippi, Black and La Crosse Rivers; the La Crosse Eagle near Riverside Park; La Crosse Players at Main Street and Harborview Plaza; the Scroll at Third and La Crosse Streets; and Water Over the Dam
at Fourth and Vine Streets.

Did you know?
The La Crosse Players sculpture celebrates the naming of the city, La Crosse.

70. For the finest Fourth of July fireworks display on the Wisconsin Great River Road, plan to be at Granddad's Bluff for the annual pyrotechnics display. La Crosse also has an annual New Year's Eve fireworks show, the oldest community-sponsored event in the country.

Quick Facts: The fireworks are put on by the La Crosse Skyrockers, Inc. Founded officially in 1929, the non-profit group's origins date back to the mid-1800s when they were known as the Fireworks Committee. The only time that La Crosse did not enjoy its fireworks display was during World War II, when all gunpowder went to the war effort.

71. Surely, nothing could be finer than a moonlight dinner cruise, but how about one in a replica 1900s paddleboat? A sumptuous gourmet dinner is the star attraction on the La Crosse Queen as musicians serenade you and your dinner companion. Reservations are required. If you're looking for a longer stay on the water, check out the Julia Belle Swain for an all-exclusive, two-day riverboat excursion. The Julia Belle Swain also offers dinner cruises.

La Crosse Queen
Where: 405 Veterans Memorial Drive, La Crosse (Passenger loading)
Phone: 608-784-2893
Email: laxqueen@greatriver.com
Website: http://lacrossequeen.com/

Julia Belle Swain
Where: 227 Main Street, La Crosse
Phone: 1-800-815-1005
Email: info@juliabelle.com
Website: http://www.juliabelle.com/

Did you know?
In the mid-1800s, there were thousands of riverboats on the inland river, providing the means for commerce and prosperity for hundreds of river towns.

72. The Buzzard Billy's Flying Carp in La Crosse offers a taste of New Orleans in a relaxed atmosphere to enjoy your favorite brew and Cajun-inspired foods, like New Orleans bread pudding and blackened catfish. Sit back and enjoy an after-dinner cocktail in their 1950s-style cocktail lounge.

Where: 222 Pearl Street, La Crosse
Phone: 608-796-2277
Website:
http://www.buzzardbillys.com/vnews/display.v/ART/4522 e4904d226

Did you know?
The Wisconsin state beverage is milk, which is appropriate since the Wisconsin state domesticated animal is the dairy cow.

73. Look to the stars at the University of Wisconsin-La Crosse Planetarium. Located in Cowley Hall, the planetarium offers public programs during the spring and fall, as well as their own Album Encounter shows on Friday evenings during the school year. These multi-media and laser light shows bring music to a new plan.

Where: Northwest corner of East Avenue and Pine Street, La Crosse
Phone: 608-785-8669
Website: http://www.uwlax.edu/planetarium

Quick Fact: There are 88 known constellations visible in our skies, each with a story rich in Greek mythology.

74. Grab the wheel and pilot your own overnight houseboat on the Mississippi River. For extended stays on the river, rent a fully-equipped deluxe houseboat at Huck's Houseboat Vacations, complete with a hot tub, flying bridge and party top on every houseboat.

Where: South Bay Marina, 699 Park Plaza Drive, La Crosse
Phone: 920-625-3142
Website: http://www.hucks.com/

"Do you know what it means to be a boy on the banks of the Mississippi, to see steamboats go up and down the river, and never had a ride on one? Can you form any conception of what that really means? I think not."

~Mark Twain from an interview in the September 7, 1902 issue of *New York World*

Stoddard

75. For a great old-fashioned Wisconsin supper club meal, dine at Rocky's Supper Club in Stoddard, WI. The restaurant's Creamy Bacon Zinger Steak and the Bleu Cheese Fish are among the house specialties. Weekend reservations are recommended.

Where: 101 S Main Street, Stoddard
Phone: 608-457-2111
Website: http://www.rockysrestaurant.com/

Quick Fact: The Town that Became a River Town
Stoddard wasn't always a river town. Until 1937, it wasn't even on the river! Construction of Lock and Dam #8 flooded 18,000 acres of bottomland and brought the river to Stoddard's doorstep.

Genoa

76. Take a self-guided tour of the Genoa National Fish Hatchery. See the next generation of Mississippi River trout, northern pike, bass, bluegill, walleye, sauger and lake sturgeon in 17 open-air ponds and six raceways. Established in 1932, the hatchery is also involved with species recovery, including the endangered Higgins' eye pearly mussels.

Where: S5689 State Road 35, Genoa
Phone: 608-689-2605
Email: Doug_Aloisi@fws.gov
Website: http://www.fws.gov/midwest/Genoa/

Quick Facts: When originally platted in 1854, Genoa was known as Bad Ax City. The name came from a stream that flows into the Mississippi River about four miles downstream. In 1868, the town residents, primarily of Italian descent, changed the name to Genoa, the home town of Christopher Columbus.

De Soto

77. Visit Blackhawk Park about three miles north of De Soto for camping on the Mississippi River. The park offers camping, fishing, a sand swimming beach and picnicking facilities. During the summer, the park has a schedule of interpretative programs that explore the natural history and culture of the area.

Where: County Road Bl off of Wisconsin State Highway 35
Phone: 608-648-3314
Website:
http://www.mvp.usace.army.mil/recreation/default.asp?pagei d=152

Quick Fact: De Soto was named after the Spanish explorer who was the first European to view the Mississippi River in 1541.

78. Follow the history of the Black Hawk War on the 10-mile Black Hawk Trail, Highway B, one mile north of Ferryville to Rising Sun. There is a historical marker showing the trail where the last battle was fought.

Quick Facts: The Black Hawk War occurred with Black Hawk himself being held captive at Fort Shelby in Prairie du Chien. It was in this area that the famous American Indian conferences were held. In 1825, the Sauk and Fox nations deeded the lands east of the Mississippi River to the Americans forever.

Prairie du Chien

79. Take in a leisurely bike ride to break up your trip at St. Feriole Island in Prairie du Chien. You can pack a picnic lunch and go bird watching. Waterfowl and shorebirds are among the site's attractions. If you're lucky, you may spot a peregrine falcon on the hunt. It is open year-round, from 6 a.m. to 11 p.m.

Where: West on Blackhawk Avenue to the bridge to the island
Phone: 608-326-7207
Website:
http://www.prairieduchien-wi.gov/internal/second_level/par ks_recreation/st_feriole_island.htm

Did you know?
St. Feriole Island was the site of the only battle of the War of 1812 to be fought in Wisconsin and the last time a foreign army was on Wisconsin soil. The Battle of Prairie du Chien pitted the Americans against the British for control of Fort Shelby. Fort Shelby was a strategic site for the British hoping to get control of Wisconsin and the surrounding area. The Wisconsin-Fox Rivers connect the Great Lakes with the Mississippi River. A re-enactment of the battle is held at the island every July.

80. No trip to Wisconsin would be complete without a stop at a quintessential Wisconsin supper club. Enjoy a steak or even fried cheese curds at Jones Black Angus, Prairie du Chien, formerly known as Jeffers Black Angus. Afterward, sip a Manhattan or Gimlet at the cocktail lounge.

Where: 37640 Highway 18 S., Prairie du Chien
Phone: 608-326-2222

Did you know?
Prairie du Chien is Wisconsin's second oldest settlement. Marquette and Joliet first beheld the majestic river valley on June 17, 1673.

81. Stock up on all of your outdoor activity needs. Shop Cabelas in Prairie du Chien for an eye-popping selection of fishing equipment, camping gear and much more. If what you are looking for is out of stock, they'll surely have it in their huge catalog warehouse right next door. While there, check out their fish and wildlife displays.

Trading History: Prairie du Chien has its roots in fur trading. It began as an American Indian village and became the American Fur Company founded by John Jacob Astor. The American Fur Company had a monopoly on the raw fur trade in the 1800s.

82. Relive a decades-old tradition. Attend the Prairie Villa Rendezvous in Prairie du Chien, the largest historic re-enactment in the Midwest. Step back in time to the 1840 fur trading era with the largest re-enactment of the Midwest. It is held the second week of June. Admission is free.

Website:
http://www.prairieduchien.org/visitors/rendezvous.htm

Did you know?
Despite its sometimes bellicose past, Prairie du Chien was considered neutral ground. Quarrels were set aside as people came to the village for the spring rendezvous to exchange fur, guns and other items.

83. Historic Villa Louis in Prairie du Chien is a must see on any Wisconsin Great River Road trip. The estate, located on St. Feriole Island, was built in the 1840s by pioneer fur trader and patriarch of one of Wisconsin's most celebrated families, Hercules Dousman. The site has been renovated through the years. The present-day residence was built in 1870. The estate features original furnishings. It is Wisconsin's first State Historic Site. It is open daily April 30 to October 31. A historical marker on the site provides additional information, Waymark Code: WM5295.

Where: 521 Villa Louis Road, Prairie du Chien
Phone: 608-326-2721
Email: villalouis@wisconsinhistory.org
Website: http://villalouis.wisconsinhistory.org/

Did you know?
Villa Louis was built to be flood proof. Forty major flood events have been recorded since 1785 in the general area.

84. For an once-in-a-lifetime experience, enjoy the Midwest's most eloquent equine event, the Carriage Classic. Held annually in September, this event celebrates the passion of H. Louis Dousman and his favorite sport, harness racing. Villa Louis was known as the Artesian Stock Farm, one of the finest racehorse farms in the Midwest. It helped make harness racing the "thing to do" in the 1870s.

Website: http://www.carriageclassic.com/

Return of a Golden Age: Major restoration has been an on-going project at Villa Louis. Work was unveiled in 2002. The restoration project captured national attention. It was the subject of an exhibit at the prestigious New York School of Interior Design in 1999.

85. Learn first-hand how to prepare an authentic Victorian meal at the Servants Supper, guided by a Villa Louis cook. After your feast, take a tour of the grounds. This rare treat is offered a couple of times of a year and is by reservation only. Be sure to call ahead for the next demonstration.

Where: 521 Villa Louis Road, Prairie du Chien
Phone: 608-326-2721
Email: villalouis@wisconsinhistory.org
Website: http://villalouis.wisconsinhistory.org/

Woman's Work Is Never Done: In the late 1800s, a typical housemaid began her day at 6 a.m. and finished at 10 p.m., six days a week.

86. Delve into the history of Prairie du Chien with a visit to the Fort Crawford Museum, the second fort built in the town. Run by the Prairie du Chien Historical Society, the museum details its service as a military hospital during the Civil War. Learn about the Blackhawk War and other historical events of the area. It is open daily, May to October. A historical marker at the site provides additional history, Waymark Code: WM524C.

Where: 717 S. Beaumont Road, Prairie du Chien
Phone: 608-326-6960
Email: ftcrawmu@mhtc.net
Website: http://www.fortcrawfordmuseum.com/

Did you know?
The original fort was built in 1816, the site of Villa Louis. Its replacement occupied the site where the Wyalusing Academy stands. The fort was operational until 1856 and used again during the Civil War. The museum is the restored military hospital portion of the fort.

87. Sing the blues, or just enjoy the festivities at the Prairie Dog Blues Festival in Prairie du Chien. The festival features live music, steamboat cruises and other activities. It is held near the end of July. It is a popular event, so book your reservations early.

Where: St. Feriole Island, Prairie du Chien
Email: info@prairiedogblues.com
Website: http://www.prairiedogblues.com/

Did you know?
At the time of the War of 1812, most of the residents of Prairie du Chien were loyal to the British.

88. Enjoy historic splendor and luxury at the Neumann House Bed and Breakfast in Prairie du Chien. With cooking that *Wisconsin Trails* magazine called "sorcerous fare," you won't want to miss this magical culinary experience. It has been a family home for 10 generations. The inn features three guest rooms with private baths, decorated with antiques and traditional furniture. *Tip:* The inn has resident cats.

Where: 121 N. Michigan Street, Prairie du Chien
Phone: 1-877-340-9971
Email: theneumann09@centurytel.net
Website: http://www.prairie-du-chien.com/

Did you know?
The Mississippi-Missouri River system is the world's fourth longest river system, draining approximately 1.25 million square miles of land.

89. Get a glimpse of the fur trading industry and its impact on the economy and development of Prairie du Chien. Visit the Brisbois Store Fur Trade Museum on St. Feriole Island. Along with Villa Louis, you'll get a detailed look at 19th century life. It is open May to October.

Did you know?
The mineral, galena, created a lead mining boom, attracting American settlers to northwest Illinois and southwest Wisconsin. Today, galena is the Wisconsin state mineral.

Bagley

90. Experience our personal favorite view on the Wisconsin Great River Road at the Wyalusing State Park outside of Prairie du Chien. It is just above the location where Jacques Marquette and Louis Joliet first entered the Mississippi from the Wisconsin River on June 17, 1763. Then, you'll understand why it is called the Mighty Mississippi. While there, tour the campgrounds and pick your favorite camping spot for a spectacular "room with a view."

Where: 13081 State Park Lane, Bagley
Phone: 608-996-2261
Website:
http://www.dnr.state.wi.us/org/land/parks/specific/wyalus ing/

Did you know?
Legend has it that Wyalusing State Park is the hiding place of a buried treasure that dates back to the Fort Crawford days. Thieves made off with gold for payments to the fort. It has been said that one of the surviving desperadoes confessed that the treasure can be found "on a high bluff above the Wisconsin River."

91. Here's a wonderful way to experience Wyalusing State Park in the winter--a candlelight cross-country ski trek held the second week of February. Call the park for updated conditions.

Phone: 608-996-2261.

Did you know?
Wisconsin is from an American Indian word meaning, "gathering of the water."

92. Contemplate your place in the world as you take a short hike around the American Indian mounds located on the Sentinel Ridge at Wyalusing State Park.

Quick Fact: On a high ridge overlooking the Mississippi River sits a granite monument dedicated by nature write, Aldo Leopold, to the last surviving passenger pigeon. Read his stirring words and mourn with him over the loss of an entire species from the Earth. If you are into waymarking, this site is Waymark Code: WM1K5Y for logging your visit.

93. Here's a unique way to learn about Wyalusing's past. Take a guided night hike through the park the weekend before Halloween. Hundreds of carved jack-o-lanterns guide the way. Call the park for updated conditions.

Phone: 608-996-2261.

Did you know?
Wyalusing State Park has an active volunteer base that supports the preservation and promotion of the park and its natural resources. The Friends of Wyalusing State Park was founded in 1996. The organization assists the park in various functions, including fundraising, invasive plant control, interpretive programs and special events.

94. The Starsplitters Astronomy Club scans the universe, using their two powerful telescopes on the second and fourth Saturday nights of each month. A visit to their observatory is a great way to finish your day at Wyalusing State Park.

Email: Beverly.Pozega@dnr.state.wi.us
Website: http://www.wyalusing.org/starsplit.htm

Quick Fact: Generally speaking, the larger the star, the shorter is its lifespan.

95. How about a friendly competition with your traveling companion? See how many different species of animals you can identify as you both follow the backwaters of the Mississippi River. Rent canoes at Wyalusing State Park.

Did you know?

Clamming was a big industry in river towns, the Mississippi River being no exception. From the end of the 19th century into the 20th century, the industry prospered, providing income and jobs for its many residents. Wisconsin exhibited its wares at the 1893 World Colombian Exposition. The state's collection was later purchased by Tiffany and Company in New York.

Cassville

96. During the summer months, visit a turn-of-the-century farming community at Stonefield Historical Village in Nelson Dewey State Park. Nelson Dewey, Wisconsin's first governor, farmed this land and gave it its present-day name, Stonefield.

Where: County Highway V V, Cassville
Phone: 608-725-5374
Website:
http://www.dnr.state.wi.us/org/land/parks/specific/nelson dewey/

Quick Fact: The name, Stonefield, is a reference to the miles of stone fences on the 2,000-acre estate.

97. When traveling the Wisconsin Great River Road in the winter, stop in Cassville for Bald Eagle Days, held in January. Nelson Dewey State Park also provides excellent viewing sites from the bluffs in the park. To keep with the theme, you should also visit Riverside Park to see the eagle effigy mound. American Indians constructed the mound around 1000 A.D. The "VILLAGE OF CASSVILLE" historical marker provides more history about Nelson Dewey, Waymark Code: WM5245.

Where: Cassville Riverside Park Observatory and Cassville High School, 715 E Amelia St. Cassville
Phone: Cindy Ploessl 608-725-5855

Quick Fact: When Nelson Dewey came out west from New York, Cassville was then a part of Michigan territory.

Potosi

98. Stop by and check the incredible restoration of the Potosi Brewery. From 1872 to 1972, it was known throughout the Midwest as a producer of fine brews. Though placed on the National Register of Historic Places, the stone buildings fell into ruin. The buildings were then purchased by a grassroots citizens group called the Potosi Brewery Foundation who oversaw the restoration. It is now a restaurant and pub, serving delicious steaks and seafood. Reservations are encouraged. You can also pick up some beer or a gift to take home at their gift shop. Seasonal winter hours.

Where: 209 South Main Street, Potosi
Phone: 608-763-4002
Email: info@potosibrewery.com
Website: http://www.potosibrewery.com/

Did you know?
The Wisconsin Trust for Historical Preservation placed the Potosi Brewery on its list of 10 most endangered properties in 2002. While there, visit the National Brewery Museum in the restaurant to view artifacts and history of America's breweries.

99. Take the self-guided auto tour of Potosi. Ripley's Believe It or Not identified the town as having the longest main street in the world without an intersection. For more history, you can visit the Passage Thru Time Museum for more information regarding the area's mining history as well as the Potosi Brewery restoration.

Where: 116 North Main Street, Potosi
Phone: 608-763-2745
Email: potosihistory@hotmail.com
Website:
http://www.vangrafx.com/PTHS/museum/museum.html

Quick Fact: Potosi is the Catfish Capitol of the state of Wisconsin.

100. Put on a hard hat and go underground for a tour of a real lead mine. Originally a natural cave, American Indians worked the mine until European settlers took over the operation during the 1827 Lead Rush. The cave was originally known as Snake Cave before being renamed after 1827. The mine is open May through October, from 9 a.m. to 5 p.m.

Where: 129 South Main Street, Potosi
Phone: 608-763-2121
Email: st.johnmine@mwci.net

Quick Facts: The St. John Mine, possibly the oldest lead mine in the United States, supplied virtually all of the lead shot for the Union army during the Civil War.

Dickeyville

101. Make a pilgrimage to the grotto at the Holy Ghost Catholic Church in Dickeyville. Father Mathias Wernerus, pastor of the Dickeyville parish from 1918 to 1931, labored for five years to build the most impressive grotto and shrines in all of Wisconsin. You can take a guided tour between 11:00 a.m. to 4:00 p.m. from June 1 to August 31. Tours run weekends only during September and October. Be sure and visit the gift shop to support the upkeep of the grotto.

Where: 305 W. Main Street, Dickeyville
Phone: 608-568-3119
Email: tschultz@chorus.net
Website: http://dickeyvillegrotto.com/

The Rest of the Story: According to author, Susan Niles of the book, "*Dickeyville Grotto: The Vision of Father Mathias Wernerus,*" Father Matthias worried about the fate of the grotto. He believed it was destined to be the biggest pilgrimage destination in the country. He had concerns that the people would transform the grotto into a place "...with ice cream parlors and God knows what." Fortunately, that did not happen.

Final Thoughts

Because the Wisconsin Great River Road follows the river, you will be traveling through several areas of lowlands and wetlands. That means that some sites may be subject to seasonal flooding. The Wisconsin DNR site posts current conditions of its parks. If you are visiting a national refuge, contact the main office prior to planning your visit so you won't be disappointed.

If you travel during the fall, please be aware that some natural areas may be closed for hunting. Even city parks may conduct special hunts depending upon the game population. You should contact any conservation area you plan to visit to make sure it is open through the hunting season. In addition, some areas with national wildlife refuges are closed during breeding or migration periods.

Southwest Wisconsin has one of the higher concentrations of Lyme disease-carrying ticks in the country. If you plan on hiking, be sure and use an insect repellent containing 0.5 percent permethrin or 20 to 30 percent DEET. After your hike, check everyone--including the family dog--for ticks, which you can remove using a pair of tweezers.

While this book concentrated on Wisconsin, there are also plenty of other adventures awaiting you on the Minnesota and Iowa portions of the Great River Road that are well worth a side trip. Minnesota has the distinction of being the starting point for the Mississippi River. In Iowa, the Effigy Mounds National Monument, across the river from Prairie du Chien, is the largest collection of American Indian burial mounds in the country. You can find more information at the following website:

Minnesota: http://www.mnmississippiriver.com/
Iowa: http://www.iowagreatriverroad.com/

Above all, have fun! The Wisconsin Great River Road is a treasure to be enjoyed again and again. We guarantee that the pictures you take while traveling the road will be some of the most stunning that you ever take.

About the Authors

Chris Dinesen Rogers was born in suburban Chicago. Acting on her love of the outdoors and conservation, she volunteered with Brookfield Zoo and the Illinois Department of Natural Resources. In 1988, she moved to Minnesota to pursue a career in natural resources.

Norm Rogers ran the Mammoth Cave Restoration Camp in Kentucky, organized with the National Park Service. The organization completed several restoration projects at Mammoth Cave and other nearby caves. Chris has worked with the U.S. Forest Service, U.S. Fish and Wildlife Service and the Nature Conservancy.

In 2000, both Chris and Norm were awarded the state of Kentucky Colonel Award for their work in restoring parts of Mammoth Cave.

In 2002, she began her own art business, Weborg Lodge Studio Original Watercolors. Creativity continues to be a driving force with Chris. She started freelance writing and continues to promote conservation education.

Other Books by Chris:
"*How to Achieve Your Fitness and Wellness Potential*," Kindle Edition available on Amazon.com

Made in the USA
Lexington, KY
06 December 2016